This book belongs to

_____

This book is dedicated to my children - Mikey, Kobe, and Jojo.

Self Disciplined Ninja

Pictures by
Jelena Stupar

By Mary Nhin

I used to have a hard time staying disciplined.

As hard as I hoped,
As hard as I wished,
And as hard as I tried,
I just couldn't stay on track.
I couldn't work out why.

When I had to study for a test, I would procrastinate.

If I was trying to kick a bad habit, I wasn't very good at resisting temptation.

One day as I was walking to the beach, I wished there was a way to develop my self control.

If **X** happens, then **I** will do **Y**.

then
I WILL
DO.

y

Here are some examples...

I'm working towards going to bed earlier. So, if I have the temptation to stay up and play video games, then I will find an interesting book to read instead.

Reading always makes me sleepy.

If I want to make a better grade in my class, then I will study for 30 more minutes every evening.

If I am to be on time and punctual, then I will set my clock 15 minutes earlier than the actual time.

That evening, I went home and wrote down an If, then statement.

If I am tempted to bite my nails, then I will whistle instead.

The next day, I went to soccer practice. When things got a bit tense, I was tempted to bite my fingernails, but then I remembered what I had written down...

It worked!

From that day on, I went on to use If, then statements with many things and was soon known as the most disciplined ninja ever.

Remembering If, then statements could be your secret weapon for building your discipline superpower.

Please visit us at ninjalifehacks.tv to check out our box sets!

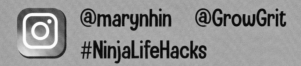

@marynhin   @GrowGrit
#NinjaLifeHacks

Mary Nhin   Ninja Life Hacks

Ninja Life Hacks